A Layman's Guide
To Vatican II

A LAYMAN'S GUIDE TO
VATICAN II

Arnaud de Lassus

TRANSLATED AND REVISED BY

Fr. Juan Carlos Iscara, SSPX, and Fr. Daniel Themann, SSPX

Angelus
Press

PO Box 217 | Saint Marys, KS 66536

Originally published as a Supplement to
Action Familiale et Scolaire, no. 221, June 2012
31, Rue Rennequin, 75017 Paris, France

STAS Editions 2012
21077 Quarry Hill Rd, Winona MN 55987

© 2019 by Angelus Press
All rights reserved.

ANGELUS PRESS
PO Box 217
Saint Marys, Kansas 66536
Phone (816) 753-3150
Fax (816) 753-3557
Order Line 1-800-966-7337
www.angeluspress.org

ISBN 978-1-949124-18-7
ANGELUS PRESS EDITION
First Printing—September 2019
Second Printing—January 2021

Printed in the United States of America

A Layman's Guide To Vatican II

As the 50th anniversary of the opening of the Second Vatican Council will be celebrated on October 11th, 2012, many conferences are to be held in most dioceses in praise of it.

How should we react to such a promotion of a major event of the history of the Church? Would this promotion be as helpful as it is claimed? To answer this question, the faithful have at their disposal many in-depth studies;[1] but these are not really useful to the Catholic general public, who have little time and whose religious knowledge is limited to the catechism.

Hence, in our opinion, the usefulness of a document on Vatican II presenting, not the whole of the subject, but only its most important aspects, allowing us to make a judgment.

Such is the object of this "layman's guide."

---

[1] Let us mention here, in particular, the acts of the nine Theological Congresses of *Sì Sì No No* and the *Courrier de Rome*, held between 1994 and 2010, and also the acts of the four SSPX symposiums of Paris, on Vatican II (2002-2005).

Contents

1. Chronology of Vatican II
2. History of Vatican II
3. List of conciliar texts
4. Qualification of these texts
5. Characteristics of these texts
6. The conciliar trilogy: religious liberty, collegiality, ecumenism
7. Opening to the world and closing to the supernatural
8. The passage from theocentrism to anthropocentrism (in other words, from the religion centered on God to the religion centered on man)
9. New notions of the Church: "the people of God"
10. Some judgments on Vatican II

    Conclusion

    Suggested Reading to Learn More about the Modern Crisis

1. Chronology of Vatican II

The Second Vatican Council opened on October 11, 1962, and closed on December 8, 1965. It comprised four sessions:[2]

—First session: October 11 – December 8, 1962.

—Second session: September 29 – December 4, 1963.

—Third session: September 14 – November 21, 1964.

—Fourth session: September 14 – December 8, 1965.

The 21st council in the history of the Church, Vatican II brought together 2,250 bishops for its opening and, on average, 2,400 for each session.

---

[2] On this subject, see the article "The Council Day by Day—Elements for a Chronology of Vatican II," in the Acts of the first symposium of Paris (supplement to *Le Sel de la Terre*, no. 43, Convent of La-Haye-aux-Bonshommes, Avrille, France). This article contains, besides the chronology, a history of the Council.

2. History of Vatican II

January 25, 1959—Announcement of the opening of a forthcoming council by John XXIII, having been pope for three months.

> It was a surprise; indeed, Pius XI in 1923 and Pius XII in 1958 had both studied, and then refused the project of a new council to complete Vatican I, suspended in 1870.[3]

1959—John XXIII chooses ten commissions and two secretariats to write the preparatory schemas for the Council. The doctrinal commission is directed by Cardinal Ottaviani.[4]

June 12, 1961—After two years of intense activity, the commissions present 70 schemas. Their number will be reduced to 20.

> This preparatory work was serious; the schemas proposed by the Doctrinal Commission were of an excellent theological clarity. But it may be already discerned, within the Central Preparatory Commission, the action of many neo-modernist prelates.[5]

October 11, 1962—Opening of the Council in Rome.

October 13, 1962—At the first general assembly, the neomodernist prelates of Germany, Austria, France, and the Netherlands act in concert (they constitute what Fr. Ralph Wiltgen, in his book *The Inside Story of Vatican II*,[6] calls "the European Alliance") and manifested themselves in a spectacular way. With their support, Cardinal Liénart asks and obtains the delay of the vote to designate the members of the ten conciliar commissions, thus affecting the future operation of

---

[3] Interruption due to the attack and occupation of Rome by the Piedmontese troops.

[4] Pro-prefect of the Congregation for the Doctrine of the Faith; a prelate of very sound doctrine.

[5] Modernism, condemned by St. Pius X (encyclical *Pascendi*, 1907), gained renewed strength after the death of this pope. In 1961, many episcopates manifested modernistic tendencies.

[6] Very important book, subtitled "The Unknown Council." [Former title: *The Rhine Flows into the Tiber.*]

the Council by ensuring that those who are selected for these commissions will be the neo-modernist Fathers of the European Alliance rather than the Fathers of sound doctrine who have had an active participation in the preliminary works of the Council.

October 20, 1962—The European Alliance obtains 49% of the seats in the 16 commissions of 24 members constituting the council structure.

> The European Alliance will succeed in obtaining the rejection of all the preparatory documents, except that on the liturgy. The remarkable work of preparation carried out between 1959 and 1962 was thus reduced to nothing.

June 3 and June 21, 1963—Death of John XXIII and election of Paul VI.

October 1963—Beginnings of an organized resistance against the European Alliance. It will take the name of *Coetus Internationalis Patrum*; to it belonged Bishop Proença Sigaud, Archbishop Lefebvre, Bishop Carli. It will become increasingly prominent during 1964.

> From 1964, Vatican II is thus characterized by a conflict between a majority group of neo-modernist prelates and a minority group of prelates of sound doctrine.

October 29, 1963—The following question is submitted to the vote of the Council Fathers:

> Whether the Council Fathers would like that the schema on the Most Blessed Virgin, Mother of the Church, be revised so as to become chapter VI of the schema on the Church?

The answer is "yes." The consequence is, according to Fr. Berto:[7]

> The disastrous vote [of October 29, 1963] departing from the gospel of the wedding at Cana, far from inviting the Blessed Virgin, had rather asked her to leave. She was a nuisance! The Virgin Mary annoyed the Council which invited her to leave. Oh! She did not let them say it twice! The earth did not shake; the lightning did not fall on St. Peter's Basilica. She left discreetly, in a deep silence; but

---

[7] Founder of the Congregation of the Dominicans of the Holy Ghost (Pontcallec); expert at Vatican II.

so discreetly that she did not say "*Vinum not habent*" ["they have no wine"]; and the destinies of the second session were sealed.[8]

October 30, 1963—Another question submitted to the vote of the Council Fathers: is it necessary to revise the schema on the Church so as to specify that the full and supreme power on the universal Church belongs—of divine right—to the college of bishops united with its head? The result is a victory for the liberals: 1,717 "yes" against 408 "no."

November 16, 1964—Paul VI adds a "preliminary explanatory note"[9] to the schema on the Church (but without rectifying the schema itself).

November 21, 1964—Closing of the third session. In his short closing speech, Paul VI attributes to the Virgin Mary the title of "Mother of the Church."

November 9, 1965—A letter-petition of Monsignor Carli in order to obtain a Council condemnation of Communism gets the support of 450 conciliar Fathers. In spite of several efforts, this request has no effect.

December 7, 1965—Final vote for the adoption of the schema on religious liberty: 2,308 votes approve it, 70 refuse it. In the conflict between the European Alliance (neo-modernist prelates) and the *Coetus Internationalis Patrum*, the modernists are victorious.

December 8, 1965—Closing of the Council.

---

[8] Letter of Fr. Berto, 1963, quoted in *Le Sel de la Terre*, no. 6, p. 169.
[9] On this subject, see below the section on the collegial structure.

3. List of Conciliar Texts

Here is the list of the 16 texts promulgated by the Second Vatican Council, with the abbreviations used:

Four Constitutions :
1. Dogmatic constitution **Lumen Gentium** [LG]—on the Church.
2. Dogmatic constitution **Dei Verbum** [DV]—on Divine Revelation.
3. Constitution **Sacrosanctum Concilium** [SC]—on the Liturgy.
4. Pastoral constitution **Gaudium et Spes** [GS]—on the Church in the modern world.

Nine Decrees :
1. **Christus Dominus** [CD]—on the pastoral charge of the bishops.
2. **Presbyterorum Ordinis** [PO]—on the ministry and life of the priests.
3. **Perfectae Caritatis** [PC]—on the restoration and the adaptation of religious life.
4. **Optatam Totius** [OT]—on the training of priests.
5. **Apostolicam Actuositatem** [AA]—on the apostolate of the laity.
6. **Ad Gentes** [AG]—on the missionary activity of the Church.
7. **Orientalium Ecclesiarum** [OE]—on the Catholic Eastern Churches.
8. **Unitatis Redintegratio** [UR]—on ecumenism.
9. **Inter Mirifica** [IM]—on the means of social communication.

Three Declarations :
1. **Dignitatis Humanae** [DH]—on religious liberty.

2. ***Nostra Aetate*** [NA]—on the relationship with non-Christian religions.
3. ***Gravissimum Educationis Momentum*** [GE]—on Christian education.

4. Qualification of the Conciliar Texts

The constitutions are obviously more important than the decrees and these more so than the declarations. Do these documents have different theological qualifications? The General Secretary of the Council, when asked which was the theological qualification of the doctrines exposed in the schema *De Ecclesia* (which would become the Constitution on the Church, *Lumen Gentium*), did not answer the question and was satisfied to quote the declaration of the Doctrinal Commission of the Council, from March 6, 1964:

> Taking into account the use of the councils and the pastoral goal of the current Council, this one defines as having to be held by the Church only those points concerning faith and morals which it will have clearly declared as such.
>
> As for the other points proposed by the Council, as they are the teaching of the supreme Magisterium of the Church, all and every one of the faithful must receive and understand them according to the spirit of the Council itself which arises either from the matter considered, or from the way in which it is expressed, according to the standards of theological interpretation.[10]

However, there is no new point concerning faith and morals clearly defined by the Council as having to be held by the whole Church.

The will to oblige the faithful being absent from the conciliar texts, the pope, by promulgating them, has not engaged his privilege of infallibility. The teaching of these texts must thus be referred to the constant Magisterium (what was always taught, everywhere, and by all). This is what John Paul II indicated on November 5, 1979, when, speaking about the "integral doctrine of the Council," he specified:

> Integral doctrine, that is, understood in the light of holy tradition and referred to the constant Magisterium of the Church herself.

---

[10] See the notifications made by the General Secretary of the Council on November 16, 1964. Their text appears in the Acts of the Council and is usually reproduced at the end of the editions of the Constitution *Lumen Gentium*.

Here are two other texts affirming that Vatican II did not define any new dogma:

> Given the pastoral character of the Council, it avoided pronouncing in an extraordinary way dogmas comprising the note of infallibility, but it has endowed its lessons with the authority of the supreme ordinary Magisterium.[11]

> The truth is that the Council itself did not define any dogma and made a point of being at a more modest level, simply as a pastoral council. In spite of that, there are many who interpret it as if it were a "super-dogma," the only one that is important.[12]

---

[11] Paul VI, November 16, 1964.

[12] Short speech of Cardinal Ratzinger before the Chilean Episcopal Conference, July 13, 1988 (*Itinéraires*, no. 330, February 1989, p. 4).

5. Characteristics of the Conciliar Texts

Ambiguous Texts

This is what Fr. Calmel underlines in his book *Brief Apology for the Church of Always*, where, talking about the conciliar texts taken as a whole, he wrote:

> It has been known for a long time that these are compromised texts. It is still known that a modernizing faction wanted to impose heretical doctrines. Although prevented from succeeding, they nevertheless managed to have ambiguous texts adopted; these texts have, for the modernists, a double advantage: they cannot be called formally heretical propositions, but, at the same time, they can be directed in a sense contrary to the Faith. Should we take the time to fight them directly? For a time, we had thought about it. The difficulty is that they do not offer a solid ground for argumentation; they are too pliable. When you try to oppose a formula that appears disturbing, you find, in the same page, another formula that is entirely irreproachable. When you seek to support your preaching or your teaching upon a solid text, impossible to be turned around, apt to transmit to your audience the traditional contents of the faith and morals, you realize soon that the text you have chosen on the subject—say, for example, on the liturgy, or on the duties of societies regarding the true religion—this text is insidiously weakened by a second text which, actually, voids the first one whereas it seemed to supplement it. The decrees follow the constitutions and the declarations follow the decrees, without offering to the mind, except with extremely rare exceptions, a sufficient hold.[13]

We find here one of the characteristics of modernist texts, thus defined by St. Pius X:

> One page of their work could be signed by a Catholic; turn the page, and you would think you are reading a rationalist. They write history: not one mention of the divinity of Jesus Christ; but when they go up to preach, they proclaim it highly. As historians, they

---

[13] Rev. Fr. Calmel, O.P., *Brève Apologie pour l'Église de Toujours*, p. 35-36.

scorn the Fathers and the Councils; as catechists, they quote them with honor.[14]

An Intentional Ambiguity

This ambiguity does not result from negligence, but from a deliberate intention. As Jean Madiran noted:

> ...the conciliar texts were supplemented (in the case of the *Nota Praevia*[15]) or even written in a sufficiently traditional way, in order to be approved with quasi-unanimity, but in a sufficiently astute way as to allow, as the aftermath showed, later developments that at the time the Council Fathers would have refused.[16]

Truths Presented with a Modernist Mentality

Monsignor Gherardini[17] explains thus this important characteristic of the conciliar texts:

> It should not be thought that there was a general upheaval. Vatican II did not innovate on all the truths contained in the Creed and defined by the preceding councils. The problem does not lie in the quantity, but in the quality [...].
>
> The rupture, before relating to specific matters, related to a basic spirit. A certain kind of ostracism had been decided, but not towards one or another of the revealed truths proposed as such by the Church. This new ostracism attacked a certain way of presenting these truths. It thus attacked a theological methodology, that of Scholasticism, which was not tolerated any more. There was a particular viciousness against Thomism, considered by many as outdated and therefore very far away from the sensibilities and problems of modern man.
>
> Nobody perceived, or nobody wanted to believe, that the rejection of St. Thomas Aquinas and his method was going to bring about a doctrinal collapse. The ostracism had begun by being subtle,

---

[14] Encyclical *Pascendi*, on modernism, § 20.
[15] *Nota praevia*: preliminary explanatory note relative to the third chapter of the *Dogmatic Constitution on the Church* (*Lumen Gentium*).
[16] *Le Concile en Question*, p. 63.
[17] Roman prelate who recently wrote two books on Vatican II—*The Ecumenical Council Vatican II: A Debate to Be Opened*, and, *Vatican II: A Debate Which Has Not Taken Place*.

5. Characteristics of the Conciliar Texts

penetrating, all-encompassing. It did not exile anybody, no theological thesis and not even certain dogmas. What it did exile was the mentality that had defined and promulgated those dogmas [...].

I wonder whether really all the Council Fathers realized that they were objectively tearing themselves away from this centuries-old mentality which hitherto had expressed the basic motivation of the life, prayer, teaching and government of the Church.

Above all, they proposed again a modernist mentality,[18] against which St. Pius X had, however, taken up a very clear position by expressing his intention: "*instaurare omnia in Christo*, to restore all things in Christ" (Eph 1.10).[19]

---

[18] Monsignor Gherardini, *Vatican II: A Debate Which Has Not Taken Place*, p. 31.
[19] The modernistic mentality is thus defined by Monsignor Gherardini:

> This Constitution (*Gaudium et Spes*) is attentive to man, as one was formerly to God. It almost replaces the worship of the Creator by that of the creature. Very concerned with the exaltation of the almost infinite dignity of the human person, it confuses the founding value with the founded value (*Vatican II: A Debate Which Has Not Taken Place*, p. 33).
>
> It is as if the program adopted by St. Pius X, starting from the formula of St. Paul "*instaurare omnia in Christo*," had been irreducibly reversed into "*instaurare omnia in homine*" as well by Vatican II as by the post-Council (*Vatican II: A Debate Which Has Not Taken Place*, p. 95-96).

6. The Conciliar Trilogy[20]

They are three errors—religious liberty, collegiality,[20] ecumenism—exposed in the documents of Vatican II [FD, DH, LG, UR, NA], between which there is a certain unity which reminds us of the revolutionary trilogy, Liberty–Equality–Fraternity.

Religious Liberty

The conciliar doctrine on religious liberty, appearing in the declaration *Dignitatis Humanae* [DH], is concerned with civil and social liberty in religious matters, that is, with the civil liberty[21] to pose religious acts in public, individually or collectively.

Summary of the Conciliar Doctrine

- The freedom to pose public religious acts individually or collectively should be a right for all religions. It is a very important right, as it is considered as the basis for all the other rights.

- The State should respect this freedom for all religions and make it to be respected. It may eventually limit its exercise according to the requirements either of the "just public order" (conciliar declaration), or of the common good (*Catechism of the Catholic Church*).

    This respect of religious liberty leads to giving a political and cultural liberty—and even a free access to the media—to the religious groups of all religions. *Cf.* article 4 of the conciliar declaration:

---

[20] On this subject, see the conference "Vatican II Summarized in Three Points," in the Acts of the 2nd Paris Symposium "Conscience in the Religion of Vatican II," October 2003, published by *Le Sel de la Terre*.

[21] By "civil liberty" we understand the immunity from constraint on the part of the State.

Religious liberty requires moreover that the religious groups should not be prevented from freely expressing the singular efficacy of their doctrines to organize society and to vivify the whole of human activity.

- The State should abstain from any discrimination for religious reasons.[22]

Opposition Between the Conciliar Doctrine and Traditional Doctrine

It is manifested, in particular, on the two following points:

- First opposition: **On the right to religious liberty**:

According to the *conciliar doctrine*

—Religious liberty (freedom to pose individual or collective public religious acts) is a right of the person, whatever his religion. This right must be acknowledged in the civil laws.

According to *traditional doctrine*:[23]

—Religious liberty (for the false religions) should never be regarded as a right, even less should it be acknowledged in the laws as a right; but it can be the object of tolerance.

- Second opposition: **On the role of the State**:

According to the *conciliar doctrine:*

—The State should not grant any privilege to the true religion (because it must not discriminate on religious grounds)

—It should not repress the false religions (unless the just public order is affected).

According to *traditional doctrine:*

---

[22] *Cf.* this passage of article 6 of the conciliar Declaration: "*Lastly, the civil power must take care that the legal equality of the citizens, which itself pertains to the common good of society, is never injured for religious reasons, either in an open or occult way, and that no discrimination is made among them* (…)."

[23] See in pareticular the encyclical Mirari Vos of Gregory XVI, the encyclical Quanta Cura and the Syllabus of Pius IX, and the encyclicals Immortale Dei of Leo XIII and Quas Primas of Pius XI.

—The State must privilege the true religion.

—It must repress the false religions (insofar as it is allowed by political prudence).

Consequences of the Conciliar Doctrine

It has introduced Liberalism into the teachings of the Church. This is what, at the time, was pointed out by an influential liberal Catholic and French senator, Mr. M. Prélot:

> We fought during a century and half to make our opinions prevail within the Church and we did not succeed. Finally, Vatican II came and we triumphed. From now on, the theses and the principles of liberal Catholicism are definitively and officially accepted by the holy Church.[24]

It resulted in almost the elimination of the doctrine of the social kingship of Our Lord. We end, thus, in a Catholicism without Christ the King.

On account of this, the Catholic States that still existed at the time of Vatican II (Spain, Italy and Colombia in particular) have now disappeared.

COLLEGIALITY

The term "college" means "*a body of persons having a common purpose or shared duties—for example, a college of surgeons.*" The term "collegial" means "*exercised by a college—for example: collegial direction.*"

By collegiality, we usually designate a form of government of the Church: the government exercised by the body of the bishops, in union with the pope, its head (this is the summit of the dogmatic Constitution *Lumen Gentium*).

---

[24] *Le Catholicisme Libéral* (1969); quoted by Archbishop Lefebvre in his *Open Letter to Confused Catholics* [Kansas City: Angelus Press, 1986]

Traditional Doctrine on the Government of the Church

The doctrine has been defined by the First Vatican Council (1870), and it is summarized by the *Catechism of St. Pius X* in the following way:[25]

> *Who is the pope?*
> The pope, whom we also call the Supreme Pontiff or the Roman Pontiff, is the successor of St. Peter in the Roman See, the Vicar of Christ on earth and the visible head of the Church.
>
> *Why is the Roman Pontiff the visible head of the Church?*
> The Roman Pontiff is the visible head of the Church because he visibly directs it with the very authority of Jesus Christ, who is the invisible head.
>
> *What is therefore the dignity of the pope?*
> The dignity of the pope is the greatest of all dignities in the world, and it gives him a supreme and immediate power over all the pastors and the faithful.
>
> *With which aim did God grant to the pope the gift of infallibility?*
> God granted to the pope the gift of infallibility so that we all could be sure and certain of the truth that the Church teaches.
>
> *When was it defined that the pope is infallible?*
> The infallibility of the pope was defined by the Church in the First Vatican Council, and if someone dares to contradict this definition, he would be a heretic and excommunicated.
>
> *When is the pope infallible?*
> The pope is infallible only when, in his capacity of pastor and doctor of all Christians, by virtue of his supreme apostolic authority, he defines, as having to be held by the whole Church, doctrines concerning faith and morals.

The First Vatican Council (Constitution *Pastor Aeternus*) specified that infallibility is a "prerogative that the Only-Begotten Son of God has condescended to join to the supreme pastoral function." In short, there is in the Church only one supreme authority, that of the pope, who is the only beneficiary of the prerogative of infallibility.

---

[25] Part I, chapter X, no. 4.

The pope may exercise his prerogative of infallibility either by himself alone, or by associating the bishops to the act in which he engages his personal infallibility.

Conciliar Doctrine on the Government of the Church

It appears mainly in articles 22 and 24 of the Dogmatic Constitution *Lumen Gentium*:

> Just as in the Gospel, the Lord so disposing, St. Peter and the other apostles constitute one apostolic college, so in a similar way the Roman Pontiff, the successor of Peter, and the bishops, the successors of the apostles, are joined together.
> […]
> In virtue of his office, that is, as Vicar of Christ and pastor of the whole Church, the Roman Pontiff has full, supreme and universal power over the Church. And he is always free to exercise this power. The order of bishops, which succeeds to the college of apostles and gives this apostolic body continued existence, is also the subject of supreme and full power over the universal Church, provided we understand this body together with its head the Roman Pontiff and never without this head. This power can be exercised only with the consent of the Roman Pontiff. (Dogmatic Constitution *Lumen Gentium*, § 22)
>
> The Roman Pontiff is […] the supreme teacher of the universal Church, in whom the charism of infallibility of the Church itself is individually present when he is expounding or defending a doctrine of Catholic faith. The infallibility promised to the Church resides also in the body of bishops, when that body exercises the supreme Magisterium with the successor of Peter. (Dogmatic Constitution *Lumen Gentium*, § 24)

Thus the conciliar text distinguishes two supreme powers in the Church:

- The supreme power of the pope acting alone,
- The supreme power of the episcopal college acting with its head.

Why speak about two supreme powers, whereas there is **only one, with two modes of exercise** (the pope acting alone and the pope acting with the participation of the bishops)? Because the conciliar process will make it possible to draw out later, from this new formulation, the idea that, in the second supreme power (the bishops with the pope), the pope would be only the President of the college of bishops.

Precision Added by the "Preliminary Explanatory Note," November 26, 1964

This Note, relative to the third chapter of the Constitution *Lumen Gentium*, recalls the traditional doctrine on the power of the pope in the Church and specifies the sense in which the term "college" should be understood:

> "College" is not understood in a strictly juridical sense, that is, as a group of equals who entrust their power to their president, but as a stable group whose structure and authority must be learned from Revelation.

Paul VI demanded the addition of this Note to the schema on the Church (which would become the Constitution *Lumen Gentium*).

How the Word "College" Was in Fact Understood

The Preliminary Explanatory Note was quickly forgotten; and the word "college" was often understood in the strictly legal sense that the Note rejected: a group of equals, which delegates its power to its president. The pope becomes thereby *"primus inter pares,"* the first among his peers; the supreme power of the pope tends to disappear.

Collegiality thus understood introduced, into the government of the Church, a form of aristocracy coming to replace the pontifical monarchy. It is, in any case, the tendency adopted by a certain number of conciliar Fathers, which they sought to impose during the Council.

> There is no doubt that some came to the Council with the intention of leading the Church into Protestantism, without Tradition (Scripture alone) and without the primacy of the pope. For the first goal, a great confusion was created; for the second, they tried to advance the argument of collegiality.[26]

---

[26] Cardinal Giuseppe Siri, *La Giovinezza della Chiesa*, Pisa 1983. Text reproduced in the acts of the 2nd Theological Congress of *Sì Sì No No*.

Such a concept of collegiality clearly deviates from the traditional doctrine, which was defined in the First Vatican Council and which was recalled in the encyclicals of Leo XIII (in particular *Satis Cognitum* of June 29, 1896).

ECUMENISM[27]

The dictionaries usually define ecumenism as being a *"movement favorable to the reunion of all the Christian Churches into one."* The word indicates, in fact, at the same time, a movement, a behavior, and a doctrine. To this ecumenism is devoted the conciliar decree *Unitatis Redintegratio* [UR].

Traditional Doctrine on the Unity of Christians

It is explained in, among other documents, the encyclical *Mortalium Animos* of Pius XI, January 6, 1928, and in the instruction on the ecumenical movement, promulgated by the Holy Office on December 20, 1949.

It can be summarized in the following points:

1. "The Catholic Church has the plenitude of Christ" and does not have to be perfected by the contributions of the other confessions.
2. Union should not be pursued by attempting a progressive assimilation of the various professions of faith nor by means of an adaptation of Catholic dogma to some other doctrines.
3. The only true union of the Churches can be done by the return (*per reditum*) of the separated brethren to the true Church of God.[28]
4. Those formerly separated who now return to the Catholic Church do not lose anything of what was still authentically Christian in their former confession, but find it, on the

---

[27] Issue covered in particular in the book of Romano Amerio, *Iota Unum* [Sarto House, 1998].

[28] See this passage in the encyclical *Mortalium Animos* of Pius XI: "*The union of the Christians can be procured only by supporting the return of the dissidents to the one and true Church of Christ, that they have had the misfortune of abandoning.*"

contrary, in a complete and perfect dimension ("*completum atque absolutum*").[29]

Two points are to be noted:

- There is a **fundamental inequality** between the Catholic Church, which possesses the truth and the apostolic succession, and the other Christian confessions, which have neither the one nor the other.
- The desired union supposes a fixed center (the Church of Rome) and a **return of the "separated brethren" to this center.**

Conciliar Doctrine on the Unity of Christians

Ecumenism as doctrine and behavior is thus presented in the Italian *Enciclopedia Cattolica* by Fr. Camillo Crivelli S.J.

> Ecumenism presupposes as its basis the equality of all the Churches regarding the problem of union. And this under a triple aspect: psychological, historical, and eschatological.
>
> a) Psychologically, all the Churches must acknowledge their equal guilt in the separation, so that, instead of accusing one another, each one may ask forgiveness.
>
> b) Historically, no Church, after the separation, can believe itself to be the only and total Church of Christ, but only a part of this one Church.
>
> c) Eschatologically,[30] the future Church, resulting from the union, could be identical to none of the Churches now existing. The ecumenical Holy Church which will emerge from this new Pentecost, will also exceed all the particular Christian confessions.[31]

The key idea of ecumenism thus defined is symbolized by the image of a broken mirror: the Christian churches (including the Catholic Church) are compared to the pieces of a broken mirror, pieces of equal value which must be gathered together to reconstitute

---

[29] Romano Amerio, *Iota Unum*.
[30] That is: from the point of view of the result to be obtained in the future.
[31] Quoted by the *Courrier de Rome*, November 1992.

the mirror which, once reconstituted, will represent the Church of the future.

A Consequence of Conciliar Ecumenism: The Loss of the Sense of Heresy

Here is a passage from the encyclical *Ut Unum Sint* (May 25, 1995) in which John Paul II took stock of ecumenism, frequently referring to the corresponding conciliar decree.

> It is necessary to pass from antagonism and conflict to a situation where each party recognizes the other as a partner.[32]

This is a particularly dangerous attitude in the case of ecumenical relationship with Protestants. Considered, from now on, as a friend with whom it is necessary to fraternize, Protestantism had necessarily to be revalued:

> Following this particularly cherished "fruit" of the Council (ecumenism), a "revaluation" of Protestantism got under way everywhere among Catholics, and certain lucid Protestants could not hide their surprise. The Council had prepared this astonishing rehabilitation of Protestantism insofar as it described, with great partiality, the religious communities resulting from the Reformation. Only the positive aspects were noticed. The ***immense evil*** that Protestantism brought upon the world and the ***aggressiveness against the Roman Catholic Church*** that even today it manifests everywhere where its affairs are not supported by the Catholic Church, all that was omitted. The Church will have to pay for this error of the conciliar Fathers.[33]

The conciliar trilogy—religious liberty, collegiality, ecumenism—characterizes well the doctrinal drift introduced by Vatican II. It was thus summarized by Archbishop Marcel Lefebvre in his book *Open Letter to Confused Catholics*, written in 1985:

> If we look carefully, it is by means of its slogan that the Revolution has penetrated the Church. "Liberty"—this is the religious liberty we spoke of earlier, which confers rights on error. "Equality"—collegiality and the destruction of personal authority, the authority of

---

[32] Encyclical *Ut Unum Sint*, § 29.
[33] Georg May, *Ecumenism, Lever of the Protestantization of the Church*.

God, of the pope, of the bishops; in a word, majority rule. Finally, "Fraternity" is represented by ecumenism.

By these three words, the revolutionary ideology of 1789 has become the Law and the Prophets. The Modernists have achieved what they wanted.

7. Opening to the World and Closing to the Supernatural

Regarding Vatican II's opening to the world, here is what Cardinal Ratzinger wrote about the influence of three conciliar texts: the Pastoral Constitution *Gaudium et Spes*, the *Declaration on Religious Liberty,* and the *Declaration on Non-Christian Religions*:

> If one seeks a global synthesis of the text (*Gaudium et Spes*), it could be said that it is a revision of Pius IX's *Syllabus*,[34] a kind of anti-Syllabus […]. We note here that the text [GS] plays the part of a counter-Syllabus insofar as it represents an attempt for an official reconciliation of the Church with the world such as it had become since 1789 […]. Only this view makes it possible to understand the sense of this strange face-to-face between the Church and the world: by "world" we understand the spirit of the modern times, opposite to which the collective conscience of the Church perceived itself as a separate subject who, after a war sometimes violent and sometimes cold, sought dialogue and co-operation.[35]

The same idea of "counter-Syllabus" is found in this remark of Fr. Congar:

> It cannot be denied that such a text (the declaration *Dignitatis Humanae*) says something materially different from the *Syllabus* of 1864 and even almost the contrary of propositions 15, 77, and 79 of this document.[36]

As they constitute a "counter-Syllabus," the three conciliar texts previously quoted are directly opposed to the traditional teaching given by Pius IX, the most characteristic opposition being "*the at-*

---

[34] The *Syllabus* accompanied the encyclical *Quanta Cura* of Pius IX (December 8, 1864). It defined itself as *"a collection, containing the principal errors of our time which are denounced in the consistorial allocutions, the encyclicals and other apostolic letters of our Holy Father Pope Pius IX."* It is an essentially doctrinal text.

[35] Cardinal Ratzinger, *Principles of Catholic Theology*.

[36] Fr. Congar, O.P., *La Crise dans l'Église et Monsignor Lefebvre*, quoted in *La Pensée Catholique*, no. 169.

tempt for an official reconciliation with the world such as it had become since 1789."

But this attempt, of which Cardinal Ratzinger speaks, goes further: it comprises a dialogue with modern thought and an adaptation to this thought, which is found to be the antithesis of Catholicism, because it is fundamentally hostile to anything that is supernatural.

8. The Passage from Theocentrism to Anthropocentrism[37]

This inversion, which characterizes Vatican II, was thus presented by Jean Madiran:

> During the Council, a Benedictine monk returning from Indochina, after only a few days in Rome gave me his impression, or his intuition:
> We have passed from theocentrism to an anthropocentrism. That is called a Copernican revolution.
> The man now at the center is not even the man of natural law. He is, on the contrary, that of the primacy of action over contemplation. And democratic calculations go before the divine Revelation. What is pastoral has become more invaluable than what is dogmatic, what is sociological overrides what is spiritual, the world counts more than Heaven. Such is "the crisis of the Church." Such is, beginning in the Church, the general de-Christianization.[38]

Here are some texts that express such an inversion:

> Believers and unbelievers generally ("*fere*") agree on this point: everything on earth must be ordered to man as its center and summit ("*culmen*").
> The Church, by virtue of the Gospel entrusted to her, proclaims the rights of man, recognizes and holds in great regard the dynamism of our time which everywhere gives a new impetus to these rights.
> (Constitution *Gaudium et Spes*)

The celebration of the Mass facing the people, which became generalized after 1969, is one of the consequences of the anthropocentrism of Vatican II.

---

[37] In other words, the passage from the religion centered on God to the religion centered on man.
[38] Jean Madiran, *La Révolution Copernicienne dans l'Église*.

9. New Notions of the Church: "The People of God"

In the above passages on collegiality, a new conception of the government of the Church was presented. This conception includes two supreme powers: the pontifical monarchy and the episcopal aristocracy—the pope being present in both, but not on the same basis.

Vatican II introduced other new notions concerning the Church, relating not to its form of government, but to its very nature. Let us mention that which is expressed in the phrase "The People of God."

Some Points of Traditional Doctrine on the Church

We recall them as they appear in the *Catechism of St. Pius X*:

What is the Roman Catholic Church?
The Catholic Church is the society or the congregation of all the baptized who, living on earth, profess the same faith and the same law of Jesus Christ, take part in the same sacraments and obey the legitimate pastors, above all the Roman Pontiff.

Precisely, what is necessary to be a member of the Church?
To be a member of the Church it is necessary to be baptized, to believe and profess the doctrine of Jesus Christ, to take part in the same sacraments, to recognize the pope and the other legitimate pastors of the Church.

Can one be saved outside of the Catholic, Apostolic, Roman Church?
No, outside the Catholic, Apostolic, Roman Church no one can be saved, as no one could be saved from the flood outside Noah's Ark, which was the figure of this Church.

Is there any distinction among the members who compose the Church?

Among the members who compose the Church there is a very important distinction, because there are those who command and those who obey, those who teach and those who are taught.

Let us retain from these quotations that the Church is hierarchical and that the membership in the Church is based on precise criteria. One is either a member of the Church or one is not; there is no half-membership.

New Notions of the Church

These were introduced by using the expression "People of God" and the term "communion," and by establishing a distinction between the Church of Jesus Christ and the Catholic Church.

- "THE PEOPLE OF GOD"

    October 16, 1963. The insertion of a chapter on the People of God in *De Ecclesia*,[39] was the work of Cardinal Suenens. According to an idea of Monsignor Philips (Louvain), it had been done to avoid the words "member of the Church" and thus to be able to include as "God's people" all Christians, those who are members of the Catholic Church and those who are not. The expression "People of God" had been rejected by Cardinal Ottaviani and his pre-conciliar Theological Commission. On October 27, in the Aula, Cardinal Siri[40] continued this criticism: "a distinct chapter can imply that the People of God can subsist and achieve some things even without the Church. That contradicts the teaching that the Church is necessary for salvation."[41]

No account was taken of the opinions of Cardinals Ottaviani and Siri, and the Constitution *Lumen Gentium* devoted its chapter II to "The People of God." The following are some extracts of this chapter:

    § 13: All men are called to be part of this Catholic unity of the People of God which, in promoting universal peace, prefigures it. And they belong to it or are related to it in various ways: the Catholic

---

[39] Schema on the Church which would become the Constitution *Lumen Gentium*.
[40] Cardinal Siri, known for his doctrinal solidity, was archbishop of Genoa. He died in 1989.
[41] Acts of the first Paris Symposium on Vatican II (October, 2002). See also Ralph Wiltgen, *The Inside Story of Vatican II*.

9. New Notions of the Church: "The People of God"

faithful, all who believe in Christ, and indeed the whole of mankind, for all men are called by the grace of God to salvation.

§ 15: The Church recognizes that in many ways she is linked with those who, being baptized, are honored with the name of Christian, though they do not profess the Faith in its entirety or do not preserve unity of communion with the successor of Peter. For there are many [...] who are consecrated by baptism, in which they are united with Christ. [...] They also share with us in prayer and other spiritual benefits. Likewise we can say that in some real way they are joined with us in the Holy Spirit, for to them too He gives His gifts and graces whereby He is operative among them with His sanctifying power.

There are three ideas in these texts:

- By defining the Church as the "People of God," its hierarchical character disappears.
- All men "belong or are related" to the Church.
- Men are united in the Holy Spirit, in a way that transcends their doctrinal divergences.

Here, not affirmed but suggested, is the idea that all men belong to the Church.

- THE DISTINCTION BETWEEN THE CHURCH OF JESUS CHRIST AND THE CATHOLIC CHURCH.

According to traditional teaching, the Church of Christ **is** the Roman Catholic Church and it alone.

In the constitution *Lumen Gentium*, no. 8, it is affirmed that:

This Church, constituted and organized in the world as a society, subsists in [*subsistit in*] the Catholic Church.[42]

This implies that the Church of Christ can subsist in other Churches other than the Catholic Church.

---

[42] Formula used also in the Decree on ecumenism and in the Declaration on religious liberty.

- ### The Concept of "Communion"

The term is very frequently found in the conciliar texts. Its meaning was explained by Fr. Congar (in 1980) in the following words:

> The concept of communion is a key concept for the ecumenism of Vatican II (…). It avoids the choice between all or nothing. We are already in communion, although imperfect, with non-Roman Catholic Christians. (…) This ecclesiology of communion has obviously not yet said its last word![43]

***

With "the People of God," with the distinction between Catholic Church, and Church of Jesus Christ and with this concept of communion, a new kind of Church is proposed here. It is no more a question of being member—or non-member—of this Church. The concept of communion *"avoids the choice between all or nothing"* and, in the guise of *"imperfect communion,"* allows multiple forms of membership.

---

[43] Yves Congar, *Le Concile de Vatican II*, Paris, 1984.

10. Some Judgments on Vatican II

Fr. Congar, O.P.

> The Church has peacefully undergone its October Revolution.[44]

Fr. Georges de Nantes

> The reforming Second Vatican Council caused, in fact, not an improvement or a new style of religious expansion, but a revolution, imposing by force a radical rupture with the past and a wholesale rejection of its centuries-old heritage.[45]

Fr. de Linarés

> (…) This subtle mixture of truths and errors which constitutes the total fact of the Council.[46]

First Paris Symposium

> Vatican II appears as a radical rupture with Catholic Tradition. Whereas the latter is wholly centered on God, His praise and service, it is not an exaggeration to consider that the Council put forward the bases for a new religion intended mainly to exalt the human person and to bring about the unity of mankind.[47]

---

[44] Quoted in *Open Letter to Confused Catholics*.
[45] CRC no. 51 (December 1971), page 7.
[46] CRC no. 50, page 5.
[47] Conclusion of the final report of the first Paris Symposium on Vatican II, October, 2003.

Conclusion

Here are some of the expressions that characterize Vatican II and which appear in the texts quoted above:
- A certain form of **closing to the supernatural.**
- The primacy of the pope contested by **collegiality.**
- The assertion (contrary to common sense) of the existence of **two supreme powers in the Church.**
- An attempt for an **official reconciliation with the world such as it had become since 1789.**
- Truths presented with a **modernist mentality.**
- A **doctrinal collapse** resulting from the refusal of St. Thomas Aquinas and his method.

When account of such data is taken, it is undoubtedly permissible to regret these words of the Holy Father announcing the Year of Faith, on October 11, 2011: Vatican II is *"the great grace from which the Church has profited in the 20th century."* This enables us to make ours the petition of Monsignor Gherardini.

> Most Holy Father (…)
> For the good of the Church, it seems to me urgent to clarify matters, by answering authoritatively the question of the continuity of this Council (this time, not in a declamatory manner, but by proposing a true demonstration) with the other councils, and the question of its fidelity to the Tradition of the Church.[48]

What to do in the face of the multiple doctrinal deviations resulting from Vatican II which have invaded the Church? The laity cannot remain silent in face of the errors that threaten their Faith. While remaining in their place as laity, they must fight these errors and, at the same time, know well, profess and defend the truths to which these errors are opposed.

---

[48] Monsignor Gherardini, *The Ecumenical Council Vatican II: A Debate to Be Opened.*

Let us reflect on these quotations, from which it is easy to draw a line of conduct:

> Whoever loves truth hates error (...): this detestation of error is the touchstone by which the love of truth is recognized.
> (E. Hello)

> An error and a lie which one does not take the trouble to denounce acquire little by little the authority of truth.
> (Ch. Maurras)

> *Error, cui non resistitur, approbatur; et veritas, cum minime defensatur, opprimitur*—Not to resist error is to approve it; and truth is oppressed when it is weakly defended.
> (attributed to Pope Innocent III)

Suggested Reading to Learn More about the Modern Crisis

Apologia Pro Tradition by Roberto de Mattei
Best-selling, powerful, well-documented, historical defense of Sacred Tradition.

The Second Vatican Council and Religious Liberty by Michael Davis
This book deals with the right and wrong conceptions of religious freedom.

They Have Uncrowned Him by Archbishop Marcel Lefebvre
Must read! The definitive explanation of the Conciliar tragedy of Vatican II.

Against the Heresies by Archbishop Marcel Lefebvre
Clear explanation of the modern errors infecting the Church based on papal encyclicals.

I Accuse the Council! by Archbishop Marcel Lefebvre
Covers collegiality, the priesthood, marriage, religious liberty, and ecumenism.

Religious Liberty Questioned by Archbishop Marcel Lefebvre
A crystal clear picture of what the Church has always taught, what the Second Vatican Council taught, and how they are contradictory.

For those new to Tradition, these books are especially recommended:

Open Letter to Confused Catholics by Archbishop Marcel Lefebvre
A study of the crisis in the Church written for all to understand.

Spiritual Journey by Archbishop Marcel Lefebvre
A Guide for life. Living as a total and unreserved offering of ourselves to God by our Lord Jesus Christ Crucified.

These titles are available from: Angelus Press, 2915 Forest Avenue, Kansas City, Missouri 64109. Order Line 1-800-966-7337. www.angeluspress.org